Light and Sound Technology

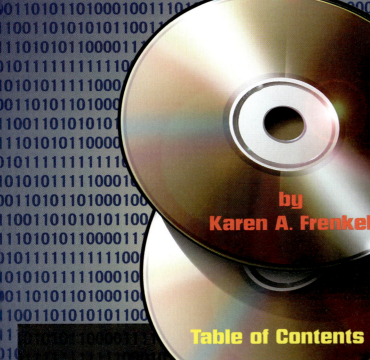

by
Karen A. Frenkel

Table of Contents

Introduction

Imagine living in a time when you could only read by candlelight. What would it be like if the only music you could listen to was live concerts? Today we have artificial light, which lets us see in the dark. Nineteenth-century inventors captured sound so that we can hear music anytime, anywhere. We often take these conveniences for granted. But 150 years ago, they were unknown.

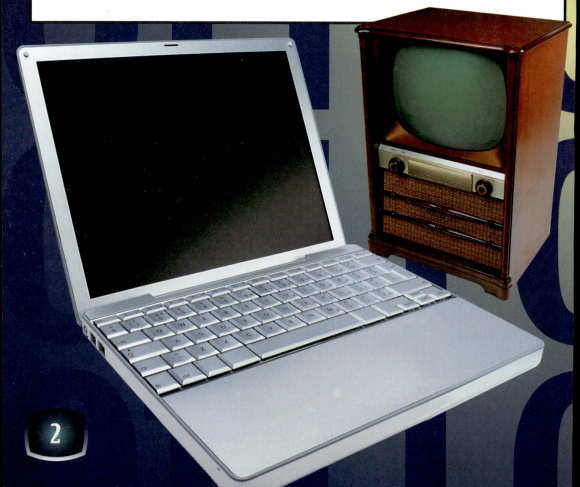

This book is about technology and science. Technology is about how science works for us.

We'll learn about lightbulbs and the first movie cameras. Did you know that televisions once had only black and white pictures? Discover the technology behind records, CDs, and DVDs. The tools and devices inventors have created changed our lives.

Turn on a light, turn down the music, and read on!

A Great Inventor: Thomas Alva Edison

Thomas Alva Edison was one of the greatest inventors in history. He lived from 1847 to 1931. He created over 1,000 inventions.

When he was twelve years old, Edison worked as a newsboy on the railroad. He got tired of selling other people's newspapers. He set up a printing press in the train. Then he created and delivered his own newspaper to passengers.

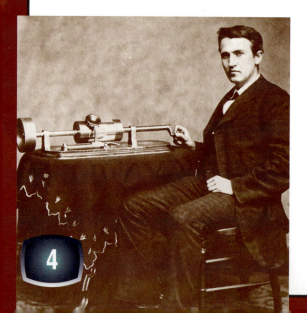

Next, Edison learned about **telegraphs** (TEH-luh-grafs). A telegraph sends messages over long distances through wires. The system could only send one message at a time. Edison improved it so that several messages could be carried along a single wire.

In his 20s, Edison became interested in the stock market. Today, we can get stock prices on the Internet. In the nineteenth century, however, people got stock prices from a ticker tape. Stock ticker machines worked like telegraphs. Edison improved the machines. With his invention of the improved ticker machine, Edison made enough money to set up a workshop.

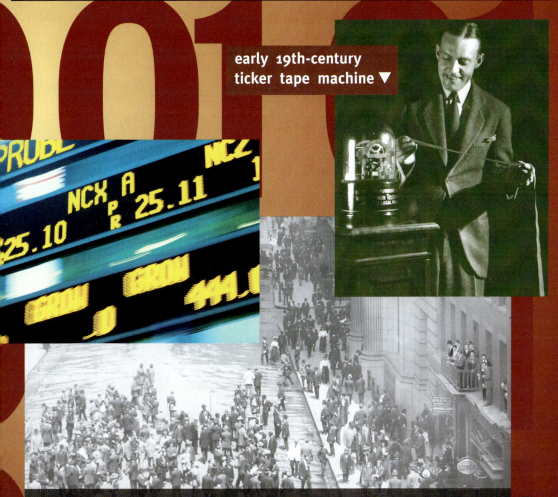

early 19th-century ticker tape machine ▼

▲ This is the New York Stock Exchange on Wall Street in New York City. People often speak of the financial markets as "Wall Street."

▲ Edison worked with a team of assistants at his laboratories in Menlo Park, New Jersey.

Edison was a success. He began to make a lot of money, but he did not stop inventing. In 1879, he invented an electric light and power system. Edison did not invent the lightbulb, though. He improved on the light globe, an early version of the lightbulb.

Edison invited 3,000 people to a party at his laboratories on New Year's Eve. When he switched on his electric system, it lit up his office, the street next to it, and neighboring houses.

This is Edison's Home ▶ Phonograph. Attached to the cylindrical record is a trumpet-shaped loudspeaker.

They Made a Difference

Edison and another great inventor named Alexander Graham Bell were rivals. In 1876, Bell invented the first telephone. When Edison heard that news, he began work on the part of the telephone people speak into. That gave him the idea for the phonograph.

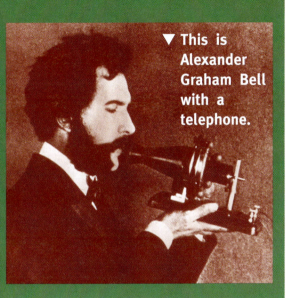

▼ This is Alexander Graham Bell with a telephone.

Edison also contributed to sound recording. He invented the **phonograph** (FOH-nuh-graf) in 1877. For the first time, people could listen to music on records.

When an inventor makes something new, he or she may want to make sure no one steals or imitates it. A patent is one way to protect an invention. In America, the inventor sends a patent application to the United States Patent Office. The office checks to see if it is truly new. If it is, the office registers the patent.

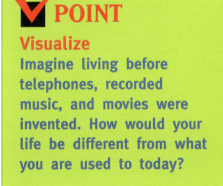

✔ POINT

Visualize
Imagine living before telephones, recorded music, and movies were invented. How would your life be different from what you are used to today?

Light Technology

Have you ever wondered how a lightbulb works? Inventors had been working on light globes for fifty years before Edison. The early light globes only provided light for a short time.

Thomas Edison had an idea. He thought he could make a light that lasted longer. He created a lightbulb with a specially coated thread, or filament, inside. The coating enabled Edison's bulb to burn for $13\frac{1}{2}$ hours. It was called an incandescent (in-kan-DES-unt) bulb. That means light was produced after electricity heated the filament.

This is a drawing for ▶ Edison's incandescent lamp. The Patent Office granted him the patent in January 1880.

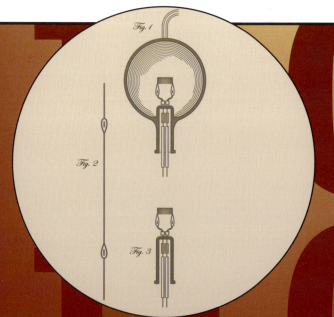

By the 1930s, lightbulbs had improved a lot. They could last for about 1,000 hours.

In the 1970s, people wanted to save energy. Makers of lightbulbs set about improving them. Today, lightbulbs require less electricity and last thousands of hours. They also produce a brighter, whiter light. They are called **halogen** (HAL-uh-jun) lamps. Car and motorcycle headlights are halogen lamps. Floodlights for stadiums are halogen lamps.

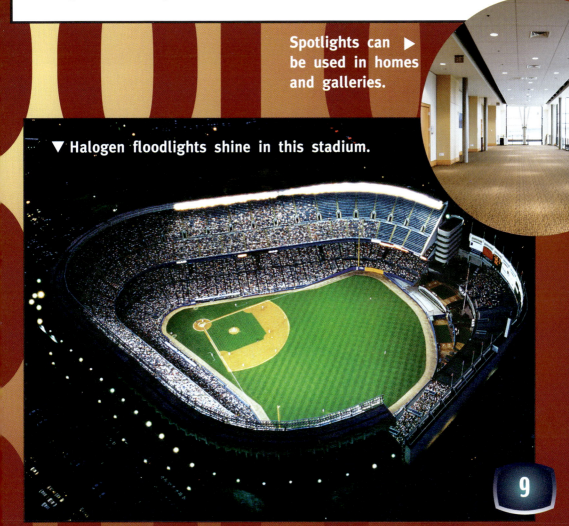

Spotlights can ▶ be used in homes and galleries.

▼ Halogen floodlights shine in this stadium.

Television

A television camera uses light to record pictures. The camera changes the light from a scene into electronic signals. The signals travel to a **transmitter** (TRANS-mih-ter). Then the transmitter sends the signals out to homes through radio waves. Antennas attached to TVs pick up the signals directly from the air. The original image is reproduced on the screen. Today, many people get signals from cable television systems or satellite dishes.

◄ The first televisions had to be very large to hold the picture tubes. Early pictures were black and white.

1. Solve This

A still image is "painted" across your television screen 30 times per second. How many times is a still image created in one hour?

MATH ✔ POINT

What steps did you take to solve the problem?

Until the 1950s, television showed only black and white pictures. Color television cameras have three tubes. The tubes split the light into red, green, and blue. The colors combine in the television receiver. The beams of light create an image by sweeping quickly back and forth across the screen. They make many thin lines, called scan lines. Think of painting an image line by line. There are 525 scan lines in each picture, or frame.

The moving image you see is really many still frames one after the other. There are thirty stills per second. Your eye blends them so that they seem to be in motion.

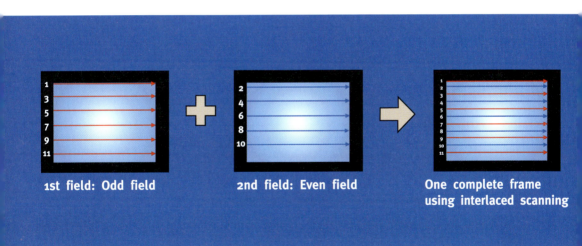

1st field: Odd field   2nd field: Even field   One complete frame using interlaced scanning

▲ The beam scans the screen twice. First it scans every other line, starting with the odd numbers. Then it scans the even-numbered lines. Together they create one still image.

Better Images and Different Screens

Television images have been getting clearer. Soon, they will seem more like movies. There is a new kind of television called HDTV, which stands for high-definition television. Sometimes it is called just HD.

HDTV screens have 1,080 lines. That's just over twice as many as the original kind.

▲ Some television programs use large HDTV screens during interviews.

Older televisions are deep and boxy. HDTVs are shallow and flat in comparison. That's because old televisions are made with **cathode ray** (KA-thohd RAY) **tubes**. Cathode ray tubes are in many devices. Video cameras, microscopes, and the scanners in supermarkets all have them.

The cathode ray tube makes scan lines possible. It dates back to the late nineteenth century. A prong, like a lightbulb filament, gives off electricity. As the electricity jumps from one side of the prong to the other, it creates a thin beam of light.

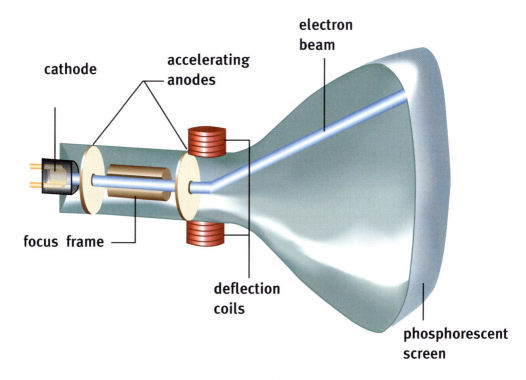

cathode

accelerating anodes

electron beam

focus frame

deflection coils

phosphorescent screen

▲ This is a cathode ray tube, or CRT for short. The screen is at one end of the tube. The electron beam scans lines back and forth.

The light shines most brightly when the tube contains no air. Another word for airlessness is a vacuum. At first, scientists could not make perfect vacuums. That delayed the development of TV screens.

By 1922, TV tubes were airtight. Many inventors experimented with them. Philo T. Farnsworth and Vladimir Zworykin were working independently at the same time. Both were able to focus the beam and create crude images. Their inventions were models of early television.

▼ Philo T. Farnsworth works on an early television set in 1928.

▲ This is Vladimir Zworykin with his kinescope. The screen was only two inches across.

In 1925, a Scottish inventor named John Logie Baird was the first to send out an image. The image Baird chose was a human face. The first sequence of images was the cartoon *Felix the Cat*.

John Logie Baird ▶

▲ This is one of the early images transmitted by John Logie Baird.

▲ This is the first image of Felix the Cat, broadcast in 1928.

Cathode ray tube TVs are bulky. They are giving way to two new display systems. One is called liquid crystal display, or LCD for short. The other is called **plasma** (PLAZ-muh) flat-panel.

LCDs change colors when sections of the screen react to electricity. Instead of creating images with scan lines, LCDs have tiny squares. These squares are called **pixels** (PIK-sulz). Each pixel has red, green, and blue filters. When electricity strikes them, they can blend into 256 shades.

◄ The numbers on this digital clock are made with a liquid crystal display.

Everyday Science

Liquid crystal displays are everywhere. Besides the newest TVs, they are on digital watches and clocks, microwave ovens, CD players, calculators, and laptop computers.

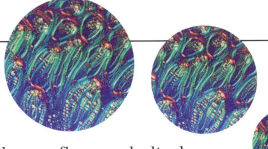

Plasma flat-panel displays also have pixels that combine red, green, and blue. Plasma is a gas. Just like liquid crystals, plasma gas changes when electricity passes through it. The particles rush around and bump into each other. When they collide, they release light.

◀ This is a microscopic liquid crystal. It is colorful because it bends light in many different directions.

HDTVs are sleek and thin because they use these new screen technologies.

▼ This is a high-definition television, or HDTV.

17

Recording Television Shows

Can you imagine a world in which you could only watch a show once? That is what it was like before videotape recorders.

The first videotape recorder was invented in 1948. The recorders wound tape on large wheels called reels. In the 1970s, **cassettes** arrived. A cassette was the size of a paperback book. Cassettes were smaller and more convenient than the reels.

✓POINT
Make Connections
How do people use videocassettes at home? At school? At work?

▲ This videotape recorder was made in 1966.

In the 1980s, engineers invented a new way to record sound: the compact disc, or CD for short. The CD led to digital video discs (DVDs), which hold both images and sounds.

◀ These are two of the first videocassette players.

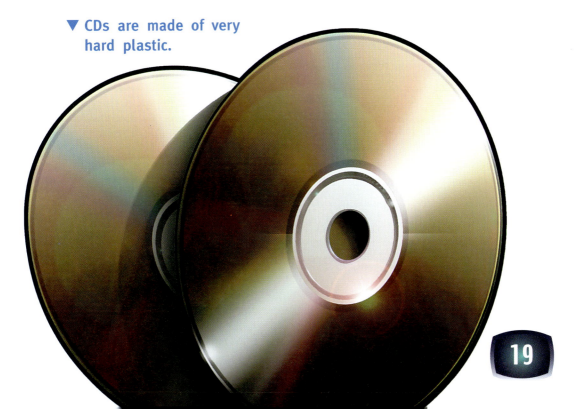

▼ CDs are made of very hard plastic.

Sound Technology

Let's go back to a time before music was recorded on CDs. When Edison invented the phonograph, he recorded sound onto **cylinders** (SIH-lun-derz). Cylinders are shaped like tubes. He covered his cylinders with tin foil. Then he placed a needle on the foil and turned the cylinder. When sound made the needle jiggle, it scratched grooves in the foil. To play the sound back, another needle traced the grooves.

2. Solve This

CDs hold up to 80 minutes of music. DVDs hold up to 488 minutes of music. How many more hours and minutes of music do DVDs hold?

MATH ✔ POINT

How did you get your answer?

Over the years, cylinders gave way to records. The first records turned at 78 revolutions per minute. They only held about 3 or 4 minutes of sound. Later records turned at 33½ revolutions per minute. These were called "long-playing" records and held about 30 minutes of sound. When people say they listened to "78s" and "LPs," they mean those early records.

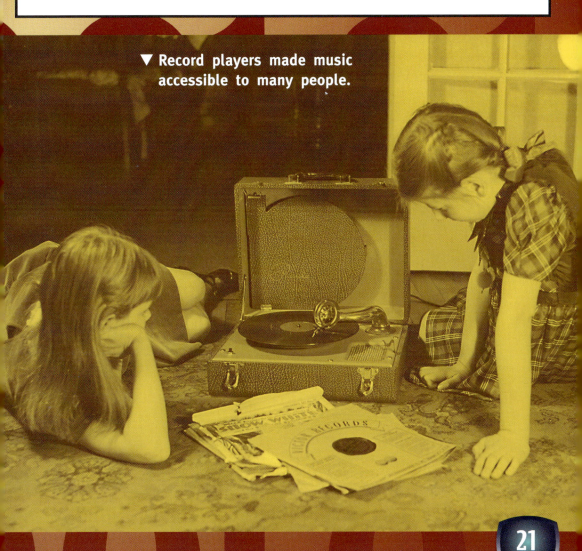

▼ Record players made music accessible to many people.

Audiotape is another way of recording sound. The sound gets converted into electronic signals. The electronic signals are stored on magnetic tape.

Like videotape, early audiotape wound around large wheels. Then, in 1963, audiocassettes were introduced. One way they are different than records is that you can stop or eject them in the middle of a song.

▼ Audiocassettes were popular in the 1960s.

Audiotapes have to be wound forward or backward to find a song. Songs cannot be played in any random order. Audiotapes also have background noise.

CDs arrived in the 1980s. Instead of a needle, CD players use a very strong beam of light to "read" the information on CDs. The beam of light is called a **laser** (LAY-zer). Lasers are very powerful tools. They can cut through metal, are used for surgery, and can carry telephone signals.

Everyday Science

Have you ever wondered how supermarket checkouts work? Most packages have a label with a bar code. The bar code has rows of lines and numbers. The cashier drags packages across a window so that a laser can read the bar code. The laser sends the price information to the cash register.

2 0 5 2 0 5 2 0 5 2 0 5

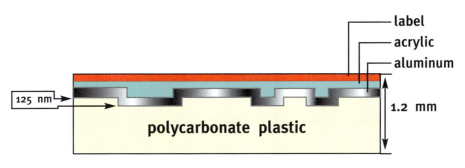

label
acrylic
aluminum

125 nm

1.2 mm

polycarbonate plastic

▲ This is a large side-view of a CD with tiny pits.

23

CDs are made of a very strong plastic. They are harder to break or scratch than records. You can make them play songs in any order. CDs turn at 500 revolutions per minute.

3. Solve This

LPs hold 30 minutes of music. New CDs hold 80 minutes. LPs were invented in 1930. CDs were invented in 1980. How many more minutes of music do today's CDs hold as compared to LPs? How many years did that increase take?

MATH ✔ POINT

What steps did you take to solve the problem?

Over the years, people have wanted to travel with their music. The Walkman was the first invention that enabled people to listen to audiotapes on a small, highly portable device.

The latest miniature music player is the MP3 player. Songs on MP3 players are stored as computer files. The files of music are called MP3s. People can buy their favorite songs as MP3 files from stores on the Internet. Then they can transfer the files to their players. People can also copy music from CDs onto MP3 players.

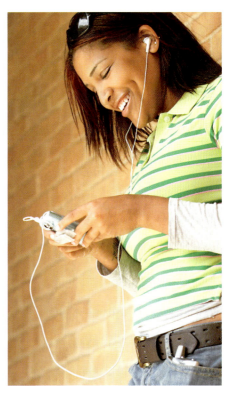

▲ This boy is listening to music on a portable CD player.

▲ This girl is listening to music on an MP3 player.

25

Computers and the Future

Computers can store large amounts of **data** (DAY-tuh). The information is stored on the hard drive of a computer. People use computers to listen to music and watch TV shows and movies. Today's computers can hold thousands of songs or hundreds of DVDs. We could not listen to music or watch DVDs on an early computer. The amount of memory was much too small.

4. Solve This

There are 8 bits to a byte. How many bits are there in 500 bytes?

MATH ✔ POINT

How did you solve the problem?

▲ Data is stored in the hard drive of a computer.

Computers are getting smaller and more powerful all the time. It's even possible to watch a movie using the tiny computer inside some cell phones!

Conclusion

Televisions and computers are becoming more and more alike. Some computers have built-in television tuners. The Internet is a resource for people who want to listen to music and watch clips of video. People also use computers to play video games.

You can use your computer to be very creative. You can send and receive e-mail, make your own cartoons, and even produce movies on your computer. We say computers are multimedia devices because they allow people to be creative in so many different ways.

Computers will do many other things in the future. They may control the appliances or the heating and cooling systems in your home, for example. What might your future computer be able to do?

▼ Someday, the appliances or the heating and cooling systems of your home might be run by a computer.

Time Line

1847   Thomas Alva Edison is born.

1876   Alexander Graham Bell invents the first telephone.

1877   Edison invents the phonograph.

1879   Edison invents an electric light and power system.

1880   Edison gets a patent for the lightbulb.

1910s   Records are made.

1925   John Logie Baird becomes the first person to transmit moving images.

1929   Vladimir Zworykin patents his kinescope, a TV camera tube.

1931   Thomas Alva Edison dies.

1953   A successful color television system begins commercial broadcasting on December 17.

1982   CDs are introduced.

1991   MP3 players are introduced.

Solve This Answers

1. Page 10
108,000 times per hour
60 seconds/minute x 60 minutes/hour =
3,600 seconds/hour
3,600 x 30 = 108,000

2. Page 20
6 hours, 48 minutes
488 – 80 = 408 minutes
408 ÷ 60 = 6 hours, 48 minutes

3. Page 24
50 more minutes; 50 years
80 – 30 = 50 minutes
1980 – 1930 = 50 years

4. Page 26
4,000 bits
500 x 8 = 4,000

Glossary

cassette   (kuh-SET) a plastic case that holds two reels of audiotape or videotape (page 18)

cathode ray tube   (KA-thohd RAY TOOB) a tube in televisions that creates scan lines on a screen (page 13)

cylinder   (SIH-lun-der) a tube-like shape (page 20)

data   (DAY-tuh) information (page 26)

halogen   (HAL-uh-jun) a lamp that gives off very white light (page 9)

laser   (LAY-zer) a powerful beam of light (page 23)

phonograph   (FOH-nuh-graf) an early record player that produces sound through the use of a needle that traces grooves on a disk (page 7)

pixel   (PIK-sul) the smallest part of the screen on a television or computer monitor (page 16)

plasma   (PLAZ-muh) a gas that changes when electricity passes through it (page 16)

telegraph   (TEH-luh-graf) a device that sends messages over long distances through wires (page 4)

transmitter   (TRANS-mih-ter) the part of a TV camera that sends pictures through radio waves to homes (page 10)

Index